ROMSEY

YESTERDAY AND TODAY

by
Barbara Burbridge
and
Gerald Ponting

Millers Dale Publications

Published 1999 by
Millers Dale Publications
7, Weavers Place, Chandler's Ford, Eastleigh, SO53 1TU
in association with
Lower Test Valley Archaeological Study Group
Romsey

MDP web-site - http:\\home.clara.net/gponting/index-page22.html

Cataloguing-in-Publication Data
A catalogue record for this book is available from the British Library

ISBN : 0 9517423 4 5

Printed by
Hobbs the Printers, Totton, Hants

Front cover photograph :
Romsey town centre, from a picture postcard
of the early 1900s (see caption to picture 3)

CONTENTS

While many readers may simply enjoy comparing the photographs, this book has been arranged in a sequence which may, if the reader wishes, be followed as three distinct walks. Each walk starts and ends at the Market Place. The map and directions at the back of the book should help as a guide.

A tour of Romsey Abbey, a walk to Greenhill and a visit to Broadlands, however, must be seen as optional extras in terms of time and effort. It is also necessary to ascertain if Broadlands is open on any particular day.

Note : only the numbers of the historic photographs have been listed here. In most cases, the photograph on the facing, right-hand, page has been taken from the same spot in 1999.

INTRODUCTION

Romsey has a long history stretching back into prehistoric times. It developed on a platform of firm dry land, which provided an island refuge amongst the surrounding waterways and marshes of the lower Test Valley. This site attracted people during the Late Bronze Age and Early Iron Age. Significant finds relating to these prehistoric people have been located on the lower end of the 'island', near and to the south of Romsey Abbey. Evidence for a low-key Roman, or Romano-British, presence has also focused on this area. There is no way of knowing, however, whether occupation of the site was continuous throughout these periods.

It is likely that continuous habitation began with the mid-Saxons of the 7th century. Romsey became a centre for a Saxon iron-smelting industry, which took advantage of the nearby woodland and waterways, as well as a conveniently available supply of iron ore. Once again, the focal point was to the south of the Abbey site. In that pre-monastic era the prime settlement area may have been occupied by a powerful private, or earlier ecclesiastical, estate, its owner responsible for the smelting industry. Archaeological studies suggest that the iron-smelting lasted for several centuries, and it is possible that the iron produced was traded in the Saxon town of Hamwic (within the boundaries of present-day Southampton, some seven miles away).

The true growth of Romsey, though, is linked to the foundation of the nunnery which, according to tradition, occurred in 907AD. Just sixty years later it was refounded under the Benedictine order by King Edgar, and altogether lasted over 600 years until its dissolution in 1539. The early nuns came from royal and aristocratic families, and had great influence. As head of the community, the Abbess received many charters giving her authority and privileges; she was lord of the manors of Romsey Infra and Romsey Extra, then divided by the Holbrook Stream. Within historic Romsey Infra she had particularly strong secular powers, including the right to hold fairs and markets. The Domesday Survey of 1086 recorded four watermills under her control; at that date they would all have been corn-mills.

During the medieval period, milling at Romsey extended into the fulling of woollen cloth. Fulling was a process whereby hammers known as fulling stocks beat the newly woven cloth until it was cleaned and given a felt-like finish. With other related activities, such as the dyeing of cloth, Romsey grew to prosperity on the cloth-finishing industry. Tanning and leather-working also thrived. The market would have benefited from the affluence that came with industrial success.

As the monastic period ended, the Abbey farmlands at 'Brode Lands' to the south became a private estate. Within the town itself the people began to act on their own behalf. The first major step was the purchase in 1544 of Romsey Abbey from King Henry VIII for use as the town's parish church. The next great landmark was the royal charter granted by James I in 1607, when the town acquired borough status. During the 17th century urban Romsey developed as a centre of solid trade and commerce, still mostly linked to cloth and leather, while the outer parts, especially in Romsey Extra, maintained a broad agricultural base. The town played no major part in the Civil War, but it must have been a worrying time for the inhabitants, as Royalists and Parliamentarians vied for control of Romsey's Middlebridge, and plundered the town.

The 18th century was a period of change, initially for the worse as the cloth trade faltered. Then, the arrival of the turnpike roads in the 1750s, and the expansion of milling, came to the rescue of the town's economy. Romsey was at the hub of a series of turnpike roads, which extended the market hinterland, stimulated a coaching trade and encouraged many allied services. In the 1790s a canal was built to the east of the town. Bankers, lawyers and doctors grew in number, and, joined by successful businessmen such as mill-owners, widened the upper echelon in Romsey society. Enterprises providing for their more sophisticated tastes began to appear in the town, which saw the arrival of wig-makers and tea-dealers, amongst other novel tradesmen.

Milling technology improved, and new mills were developed. Nine major sites have been identified, most of which had ancillary activities as well as the main one. Some sites had four or five wheels in action, and this, while a symptom of success, caused considerable competition for water power. The key activities now included paper-making, leather-dressing and bark-milling for the local tanneries. Then, with the 19th century, came the processing of flax-yarn and saw-milling, the latter encouraged by the demands of the quickly spreading railway system.

The railway, however, brought no other immediate advantage to Romsey, which did not prosper during the middle years of the 19th century as the coaching trade collapsed. It was not until the arrival of the enterprising David Faber that employment prospects began to improve. He realised that the railway could be used to advantage in transporting beer over greater distances than had been previously possible, even on the smoothest of turnpike roads. In the 1880s David Faber bought up several small breweries, and, with a fine marketing sense, amalgamated them under the name of one of the brewers, Thomas Strong. Subsequently,

Strong & Co. Ltd of Romsey became a thriving concern with County-wide advertisements proclaiming 'You are now in the Strong country'.

The 19th-century economy was further improved, rather surprisingly, by the Rev. E. L. Berthon, vicar of Romsey from 1860 to 1892. He had a fascination and talent for engineering, and his main interest involved the design and production of folding boats, which he first manufactured in the vicarage garden, testing them on the adjacent waterway. As the business of the Berthon Boatyard grew, so it moved to larger premises. Unfortunately, the folding life-boats on the ill-fated Titanic, although from a different manufacturer, ruined the reputation of such designs, and the business faded in Romsey. A Berthon Boatyard continues at Lymington, but is no longer linked to the family.

Romsey at the start of the 20th century was still a small market town. Traffic conditions and other factors, however, led to the market being discontinued in the Market Place in 1919, though a cattle market was held on the site of the present Newton Lane car park until the 1960s. Romsey contributed men and effort in both World Wars, and then, from the 1940s onwards, entered into a new era with the true advent of the motor age. The car made it possible for people to live in Romsey while working elsewhere. Even with the demise of the brewery, however, Romsey did not turn simply into a dormitory town. New industrial estates offered local employment to many.

With the growth in population came an expansion in the physical development of the town. Largely prevented from spreading southwards by Broadlands Park and westwards by the River Test and its low-lying banks, new development mostly fanned out eastwards with Winchester Road and Botley Road as the main arterial routes leading to the new estates. Recently, though, there has been further expansion into the old water meadows to the north.

Since the reorganisation of local government in 1974 Romsey is no longer a borough in its own right, but has become part of the Borough of Test Valley. With the approach of the new millennium, the Borough and the Town Council are seeking to increase both the town's amenities and interest in its heritage.

SOURCES OF PICTURES

The old photographs used in this publication have all come from the Lower Test Valley Archaeological Study Group's collection of slides and prints. The modern photographs were taken by Gerald Ponting in February, March and April of 1999 (apart from Broadlands House, taken by Elizabeth Ponting in 1994).

All the photographs have been scanned and processed using appropriate computer software. The only manipulation used on the old photographs has been the removal of dust and scratches or improvement in the contrast of faded prints.

We hope that our readers will enjoy making comparisons between 'yesterday' and 'today'.

ACKNOWLEDGEMENTS

Our thanks must go first to Philippa Newnham of the Romsey Tourist Information Centre who originally suggested this book and who introduced the authors to one another.

Many people have contributed or loaned old postcards and family photographs to the LTVAS Group over the years, and the publishers would like to express appreciation for their support.

We wish to thank the Mayor and Town Clerk of Romsey and the two mace-bearers for their cooperation for picture number 8; and also Mr. B. Drummond the butcher for agreeing to match picture 32 with picture 31. Thanks also to Bob Johnson and George Kinsman for the use of a transparency scanner.

The map of Romsey, based on an Ordnance Survey map of 1867, was drawn by Jeff Hawksley of LTVAS. Other members of LTVAS have helped greatly with information, advice and proof-reading.

START
OF
WALK
ONE
Map and
directions at
back of book

1   The Market Place, c1907, looking south-east from the corner of Church Street

The Market Place has been at the heart of Romsey since medieval times. The earliest known right to hold markets was originally granted by royal charter to the Abbess of Romsey Abbey in the early 1100s; so it is not surprising that a market place developed just outside the gateway into the long-established Benedictine nunnery. The medieval market was held on a Sunday, but later changed to a Saturday, probably under 17th-century Protestant influence. In 1826 the day changed yet again, this time to a Thursday, an arrangement that continued until trading in the Market Place ceased in 1919.

2   Market Place, 1999

The overall view has remained largely unchanged during the 20th century, save for traffic conditions and several modernised shop fronts. The statue is of Lord Palmerston, Victorian prime minister and owner of Broadlands House to the south of Romsey (see caption to picture 40). The attractive building behind the statue was built about 1800, and its upper central section is faced with mathematical tiles designed to appear like bricks. During the 19th century the building was a draper's shop run by Moses Pepper, who also acted as postmaster for the town. Eventually, the Post Office took over the shop and remained there until the 1960s.

THE MARKET PLACE, ROMSEY.

Sillence, Photo Series.

3 Corn Exchange and Market Place, early 1900s, looking west

This photograph is an early version of a still-popular postcard view of Romsey town centre with the Abbey in the background. The building on the left is the 1864 Corn Exchange. Behind its tall windows was a high room where farmers traded their grain. The building was always available for hire when not in formal use, and was the venue for a whole range of activities, serving as headquarters of the Romsey Volunteers (precursors of the Territorial Army) as well as a place for exhibitions and entertainment. A 19th-century brewer, Josiah George, rented the cellars as a store, a use continued by Strong & Co. Ltd after it had taken over the George Brewery.

4   Corn Exchange, 1999

The Corn Exchange company went into receivership in 1924, and the property was quickly sold. Since then it has been occupied by many concerns including a grocer's store and a billiard room, the latter being situated in an inserted upper storey. The old Corn Exchange is currently owned by Barclays Bank, which previously occupied only a corner of it for a time. Altogether, Barclay's link with the building has now lasted seventy years. Perhaps the most significant social aspect of this pair of photographs, apart from the obvious differences in dress and traffic, is the total lack of interest shown towards the modern photographer.

Corn Market, Romsey.

5   The Cornmarket, **early 1900s, looking west**
The left side of the wide space called the Cornmarket was once the southern boundary of a huge medieval market place before infilling separated it from the main market area. It takes its present name from the Corn Exchange, seen on the right, but was previously called the Pig Market, probably after the many butcher's shops in the vicinity. Records of Romsey's Court Leet, from the 1700s and early 1800s, detail many complaints about negligent butchers, who left their chopping blocks out on the thoroughfare. The presence of so many men in this photograph, together with the hurdle pen in front of the Corn Exchange and a calf standing in the group on the left, suggests that it was taken on a market day.

6   The Cornmarket, 1999

The Cornmarket was pedestrianised in 1996. Since then it has become the focus for special events and entertainments with provision for outdoor refreshments during the summer months. An upper floor, inserted into the Corn Exchange around 1929, made new windows necessary. The roof pediment, however, remains with the inset pitchfork, sheaves and sickle symbolising the building's original main purpose. The horse trough in front of the old Corn Exchange was given to the town in 1886 by Lord Palmerston's heir, the Rt Hon. William Cowper-Temple, MP, later Lord Mount Temple. He and his wife were devoted to the cause of animal welfare. The facade of the *Dolphin Hotel* on the left underwent major restructuring in 1828. Romsey's market continues only as a collection of stalls in the *Dolphin* yard on Fridays and Saturdays.

7   Aldermen of the Borough of Romsey, outside the Town Hall in 1959

In 1607 King James I granted borough status to Romsey. His charter confirmed a town council comprising a mayor, twelve aldermen and twelve burgesses, supported by a town clerk - to be 'a prudent and upright man' - two sergeants-at-mace and a recorder to run the court. There had been mayors of Romsey from at least the 1430s. Until the dissolution of Romsey Abbey in 1539, though, they operated under the auspices of the Abbess as lord of the manor. The 1607 charter marked the start of a true corporate identity. This photograph shows members of the 1959 Corporation outside Romsey's Town Hall, on the south side of the Market Place, on the occasion of the presentation of the freedom of the Borough to the Hampshire Regiment.

8   Mayor, Town Clerk and Mace-bearers, 1999
Romsey ceased to be a borough with the local government re-organisation of 1974, when it became part of the Borough of Test Valley. Although the Town Council now only has the powers of a parish council, the mayoralty has been retained as a result of intervention by Lord Mountbatten at the time of re-organisation. Here the senior mace-bearer (Mr Peter Pearl), the town clerk (Mrs Kate Bunce), the 1998-9 Romsey town mayor (Cllr Max Buckmaster) and the junior mace-bearer (Adam Spurling) stand once again outside the Town Hall prior to their departure for the St George's Day parade (18th April 1999).

9   Romsey Volunteers, outside the Town Hall in the Market Place, c1908
Volunteer part-time soldiers have long provided the country with a form of home defence. Crises, such as the Napoleonic Wars, always inspired an increase in membership. At other times, changes to name and uniform were favourite ploys to encourage new recruits. The Romsey Volunteers' band was particularly popular, and performed at many varied functions. After 1908 the Volunteers were disbanded, and many transferred to the newly formed Territorial Army. This picture may illustrate the last parade of the Romsey Volunteers.

10   Postcard message

The modern view of this part of Romsey's Market Place may be found in picture 12. It seemed more appropriate here to reproduce the message on the back of the picture postcard (opposite). It reads: *Dear Walter, I thought you would like this PC - it's the Volunteers presenting the Colours to the Romsey Corporation when we came back from Church on Easter Sunday morning. You will find some of us out especially Capt Footner & Billy Holloway with the child in his arms. It was a lovely morning & we are going to hang the colours in the Council Chamber with the old flags. You know where I mean. So goodbye to both of you. Your Affectionate Dad/?Adieu*

11 The Abbey Gateway and the west side of the Market Place, c1898

This picture was taken after the Abbey gateway was rebuilt in 1888 (as part of the Congregational Church; now United Reformed Church) and before Lloyds Bank was built. Sawbridge's was a short-lived business in the premises. Before Mr Sawbridge's time the building had been occupied for several decades by Lordan's the printers. Christopher Legge Lordan was mayor of Romsey when the present Town Hall was opened in 1866, and his initials 'C.L.L.' are over the doorway of that building.

12   Lloyd's Bank, 1999

Lloyds Bank was built on the site of Sawbridge's in 1900. An interlaced monogram of the date may be seen on the south wall near the gateway. The bank was later extended northwards, taking over the shop belonging to John Tuck, silversmith and clockmaker. The clock on the wall is over the barely noticeable join, and is a reminder of the clock on Mr Tuck's shop front.

13   Abbey Water, looking west, early 1900s

Abbey Water is a turning to the left just before the Abbey gateway; it is the name of both the road and the water that runs there. It once marked the southern boundary of the medieval monastic precinct. The waterway also long served as the mill-pond for the mill known as Abbey Mill, seen in the background of this picture. Though the site of this corn-mill changed slightly, probably three times, it can be traced back to 1551. The final mill building, which can be seen at the end of the road, burnt down in 1925.

14   Abbey Water, 1999

With the mill gone and the water narrowed and railed in, the mill site was absorbed into the Convent of La Sagesse, established in 1888. The left-hand properties date from various periods. The small end-on terrace behind the lamp-post provided homes for 18th-century mill-workers. The oldest of the far white-fronted houses was built in the 1790s by Thomas Maunder, a cabinet-maker; the corner section is probably a mid-Victorian extension. The central building on the left is essentially timber-framed, despite its brick facade, and is the oldest along the entire row. It may be the property referred to as 'the Bowleing green house' in a deed of 1722, and later called 'Hewletts' after a family that lived there for some time.

15   Romsey Abbey, from the south-east, c1880

Romsey Abbey was the church of the Benedictine nuns, whose community survived from the early 10th century until the dissolution in 1539. This Abbey church, thought to be the third on the site, took about 130 years to build between 1120 and 1250, when the nunnery was probably at its peak with nearly 100 nuns. After the Black Death, in 1348, there were never more than about 25 nuns, who were mostly of lower status than in earlier times. Many changes have taken place over the centuries, some quite small. In this picture the Abbey has a square clock, while much of the Abbey's present south garth is part of a private garden complete with greenhouse.

16   Romsey Abbey, 1999

Since the end of the 1800s the tower has boasted a round clock. In the early part of the 20th century Colonel Wilfrid Ashley of Broadlands bought the garden area and restored it to the Abbey. During the time of the nunnery this south side was within the nuns' secluded area, protected by boundary walls. The cloisters adjoined the wall of the south aisle, stretching along from the corner made with the south transept. The nuns' domestic quarters were to the west and south. The townspeople, meanwhile, had the use of the north aisle as their parish church, subsequently extended to include the north transept. This church-within-a-church was separately dedicated to St Lawrence. In 1544 the townspeople bought the entire church building from Henry VIII for £100. The Abbey Church became the Parish Church, a purpose that it has served to the present day.

17   Romsey Abbey interior, looking east, c1904

Like most large stone buildings, the 12th-century Romsey Abbey has been notoriously difficult to heat. In the 1860s the vicar of Romsey, Rev. E. L. Berthon, introduced Gurney stoves like the one seen in the left foreground. He also lowered one of the east windows to make it even with the other. These east windows had been inserted rather haphazardly after being removed from their original position in a two-bayed lady chapel, pulled down centuries earlier. Rev. Berthon died in 1899, and a stained-glass window in his memory may be seen in the north transept. It commemorates his involvement with boat-building and astronomy as well as his dedication to the church.

18   Romsey Abbey interior, 1999
The Gurney stoves have gone, but a new feature has appeared in the form of loudspeakers on the columns. The screen, across the chancel steps in the old photograph, has now been resited between the nave and the north transept. The screen was reconstructed from a medieval fragment discovered by the Rev. Berthon, who placed it in its earlier position. The chapel in the north transept, beyond the present line of the screen, is still dedicated to St Lawrence, patron saint of the medieval parish church. Romsey Abbey is dedicated to St Mary and St Ethelfleda.

Band Concert.
Memorial Park, Romsey.

Silpho Series

19   The Town Memorial Park in its early years

The Town Memorial Park is to the west of the Abbey gateway, at the end of the road called The Meads; it is in a low-lying area beyond the one-time Abbey precinct. The land, bordered by swiftly flowing waterways and tapering away towards the River Test itself, required extensive drainage work. The park was then created to commemorate the fallen of the First World War, and opened in 1921. The stone memorial is a focal point within it. The thatched bandstand was an attractive feature, and regular band concerts were popular for many years.

20   The Town Memorial Park, 1999

The park, with its colourful floral displays, remains popular. Tennis courts, a bowling green, children's play area, refreshment kiosks and attractive walks appeal to people of all ages. The park's war memorial now also records those who fell in later conflicts, while the bandstand has been replaced by the Japanese gun brought back from the Far East by Lord Mountbatten of Burma. The gun or 'cannon' was officially given in tribute to Romsey's war effort; it has also provided a tempting climbing frame for several generations of local children, though it is now in too dangerous a condition for this activity to be considered safe.

Sadlers Mill Romsey.

F.E.Sillence,Photo.

21   Sadler's Mill from a postcard posted on 3rd August 1910

There has been a mill site here on the main River Test since the early 16th century at least. At that time it was the subject of considerable discord as rival millers upstream tried to divert water to their advantage. The surviving mill building was built in 1747 by the then owner, the first Lord Palmerston of Broadlands. The miller's house, on the left, was added in the 1770s. In the early 1900s the mill-house became a small private school run by Miss Fanny Buckell, the splendidly eccentric daughter of a local doctor. One of her pupils later recalled with amusement how her parents thought that she should get used to 'the rough and tumble' of school life: there were just five other children in total ! Two of the six grew up to become mayors of Romsey.

22   Sadler's Mill, 1999
The spit of land has disappeared, while today there is a tree in the foreground. This is one of Romsey's favourite beauty spots, often called 'The Salmon Leap' because each autumn the salmon have long tried to leap upstream to their breeding grounds. After several changes of ownership, Sadler's Mill is once again part of the Broadlands Estate. In the mill's final active role, a turbine-driven generator was installed to produce electricity for much of the estate. Since the 1960s, though, the mill has fallen into disuse.

23   Romsey from Greenhill, early 1900s

Greenhill, on the west side of the Test Valley at Romsey, edges in slightly towards the river and the ancient township. It has long been a popular walking destination from Romsey, and many photographers and artists have captured the scene from the hill, looking over the River Test to the town. The size of Romsey Abbey is very noticeable in this distant view, dwarfing another substantial building just in front of it. This is Rivermead House, a mill-owner's house (opposite the gates of the Town Memorial Park). The soaring chimney of the old leatherboard mill may be seen to its left.

24   Romsey from Greenhill, 1999

There has been only a little growth of the town towards Greenhill. New developments have been mostly eastwards towards Winchester and, more recently, northwards onto the old water-meadows. The 'Greenhill' view, therefore, remains largely unspoilt. The 'leatherboard' chimney has gone, however, and Rivermead House now serves as offices. Also, a larger modern agricultural building has replaced the barn and traditional hayrick seen in the older photograph.

25   Middlebridge, early 1900s, viewed from the Causeway to Sadler's Mill

This elegant single span-bridge was built in the 1770s. Thanks its height, it was possible to see Broadlands House under its arch. Its predecessor had been a two-span stone bridge, reported as being in poor condition by the early 1600s, long before it was replaced by the one in this photograph. The earlier bridge was the scene of a Civil War skirmish, as the Royalists and Parliamentarians contested this important crossing point. Perhaps unexpectedly, the two sons of Henry St Barbe, then owner of nearby Broadlands, fought on the side of Parliament against King Charles I. Although John survived the war, Francis St Barbe was fatally wounded at the first battle of Newbury in 1643.

26   Middlebridge, 1999

Middlebridge was rebuilt on the same foundations as part of the Romsey by-pass construction in the 1930s. This early by-pass probably saved the town from over-zealous town-planning in the 1960s, when some people argued for the redevelopment of the old streets. The modern bridge is in the same style as, but much flatter than, its 18th-century predecessor. It is the third known 'middle' bridge, though records reveal that there has been a bridge at this crossing point since the 13th century at least. These records are not helpful, however, in determining exactly what the bridge was considered to be in the middle of ! Today, in this view, it marks the boundary between Broadlands Park to the south and the western edge of Romsey to the north. For travellers crossing the bridge it leads them from town to country.

Middlebridge Street, Romsey.

5469.

27   *The Three Tuns*, Middlebridge Street, looking northwards, c1910

The Three Tuns greeted travellers from the west in the days when Middlebridge Street carried all the traffic going to and from the great river crossing at Middlebridge. The building reputedly dates from the early 17th century, and its use as a pub has been traced to the 18th century. The Holbrook stream flows under the forecourt. The high building in the background began as a wool warehouse, an echo of Romsey's medieval cloth-finishing industry. Tanneries also dominated this area, making good use of the available water until the early 20th century. The entrance to the last one was just beyond the lamp-post on the right.

28 Middlebridge Street, 1999

A 1990s residential development on the site of the old tannery, though only glimpsed in this photograph, has given a new ambience to the lower part of Middlebridge Street, but *The Three Tuns* remains a constant focal point, as does the old warehouse, despite many changes of use. (Many Romsonians have fond memories of the old warehouse as the *Elite Cinema*.) Probably the most noticeable change to this street cannot be appreciated in a photograph. When the tanneries were thriving this was a very smelly area, with unpleasant effluents discharging into the water. Such industries were encouraged to find locations where the streams were leaving town, as is the case here.

**START
OF
WALK
TWO**
Map and
directions at
back of book

29 Bell Street looking south, c1907

The view down Bell Street was once blocked by a building that created a visual barrier between Bell Street and the other streets that continued the routes south and west. At the time of this photograph there was a rather amusing juxtaposition of names along the façade: 'The Romsey Liberal Club' occupied the upper floor, while 'Antiques' were sold downstairs. The sign of the *Cross Keys* pub draws the eye to the right side of the street. A 17th-century innkeeper there, John Bingham, left an estate of around £80, including stock-in-trade. As his horse accounted for £5 of this and his clothes for £10, he must have been a stylish individual. The soldiers in the left foreground, probably Volunteers, are enjoying a drink from the *Queen's Head*, which closed in 1911.

30   Bell Street, 1999

Before the 18th century, Bell Street was known as Mill Street because it led to the ancient Town Mill (now the site of the Duke's Mill Shopping Precinct). Then the advent of the turnpike roads brought the *Bell Inn* to prominence as a coaching inn, and the street name gradually changed to reflect this. The inn closed in the 1860s, but the building, with its decorated facade, survives as offices a short distance below the Baptist Church. The *Cross Keys* is now a restaurant, but the old inn bracket remains.

31 Butt's the Butchers, Bell Street, pre-1914

The special display of 'prize' meat was obviously considered worthy of being the subject of a picture postcard. The errand boy's bicycle on the left belongs to a life-style that has now disappeared. This corner of the Cornmarket and Bell Street was once the southern edge of the great medieval market place. The short stretch of street running off to the left, before opening out into the Cornmarket, was known as Cross Street, a name that was used in the late 19th century, perhaps with an earlier origin.

32   Drummond's the Butchers, 1999

There is still a butcher's shop on the corner of Bell Street, complete with friendly butcher, but no errand boy's bicycle is available for home delivery today. Modern hygiene regulations prevent the open-air display of carcasses – and the use of strings of sausages as decorative streamers !

33   Duke's Mill, Bell Street, 1960s

The name 'Duke's Mill' dates only from the 1930s, when it took its name from the last owner, Mr R. A. Duke. For centuries before then it had been known as Town Mill with a history going back to the medieval period, perhaps even to Domesday. Until the Dissolution of Romsey Abbey in 1539 it belonged to the Abbess. It was always a corn-mill, though in later times there were ancillary activities on the site. These included a whiting works, which processed chalk to produce the powder used in the once-common whitewash. Eventually, the mill was so mechanised and the demand on the water-power so intense that, when everything was in action, all the mill's lights would fade.

34   Duke's Mill Shopping Precinct, 1999

Duke's Mill burnt down in 1970, just a couple of years after ceasing to operate. Duke's Mill Shopping Precinct now occupies the site with only the tumbling fall of the Holbrook Stream running through to indicate the useful water-power that served the town for so many centuries. The edge of the building on the extreme left appears in both photograph. It was once the property of Josiah George, one of Romsey's 19th-century brewers.

35   Banning Street, looking south, 1950s

This photograph of Banning Street was taken in the decade before its demolition as part of the sweeping clearances so prevalent everywhere in the 1960s. The street ran south from its junction with Bell Street, just below Duke's Mill. Its history can be traced back to the medieval period when it was once known as Bannock Street. Referred to in a document of 1544 as 'the king's highway', it was probably the medieval route to Southampton, continuing on through Broadlands in the days when that property was the Abbey farmland.

36   Banning Street, 1999

The former entrance into Banning Street (from the junction with Bell Street and Middlebridge Street) has now become the entrance into Broadwater Road. This new road, however, deviates to the left after a few yards. Little remains of the line of ancient Banning Street running through the blocks of 1960s flats. Only the buildings in the background survive, notably the former *Bricklayers Arms* – the white building with the tall chimney. In the 1830s the innkeeper, Henry Floyd, must have filled the pub with his own extensive family. He seems to have been the only male member for several generations not to have earned his living as a bricklayer. At least he ran an appropriately named pub !

37   Tadburn Walk, north of the present by-pass and looking west

Before the construction of the Romsey by-pass, in the 1930s, there was only a footpath along the Tadburn from Palmerston Street towards Middlebridge. At the time of this photograph there were still a few houses along a residual part of the ancient line of Banning Street, running a short way into Broadlands: these houses show up at the rear left. The houses on the right belong to a short spur road off Banning Street known as Mount Pleasant. Further along, the Tadburn was spanned by a footbridge giving access from Tadburn Walk into Banning Street. Alongside the bridge was a ford, which remained in use until the 1940s.

38　Romsey By-Pass and Tadburn Stream, 1999
The building on the right appears in both photographs, but the by-pass now runs where the left-hand group of cottages once stood. Modern traffic has transformed this one-time quiet walk into a noisy thoroughfare, despite the attractive trees along the broad verge. Although there is still a footbridge over the Tadburn, linking the town streets to the by-pass, pedestrians today usually prefer to backtrack and walk through Broadwater Road to Palmerston Street.

39   Lord Palmerston on the steps of Broadlands, 1858

The third Lord Palmerston, the Victorian prime minister, is seen (centre, in top hat) with friends and family on the steps of his home at Broadlands. The family enthusiast responsible for such early photographs was his step-daughter, Lady Jocelyn, who married the Earl of Shaftesbury. The Broadlands Estate was originally the farmlands of Romsey Abbey, falling into secular hands after the dissolution in 1539. The first Lord Palmerston bought the estate in 1736, the only time it has been on the open market. He commissioned William Kent to improve the view by diverting the River Test.

40 Broadlands House

The second Lord Palmerston was responsible for converting Broadlands House into the elegant Palladian mansion that is seen and enjoyed today. He employed Capability Brown to design the grounds and, more unusually, also involved him in the design of the new house. Broadlands is open to visitors in the summer months, along with a major exhibition about its more recent resident, Earl Mountbatten.

Lord Palmerston's statue, 1999

The third Lord Palmerston died in 1865. This statue in his memory was erected in the Market Place in 1868. It is the work of London sculptor, Matthew Noble. The position of the statue is appropriate as Lord Palmerston kept a very close interest in Romsey affairs. Just before his death he was involved in the plans for the nearby Town Hall, but unfortunately did not live to see it opened in 1866. The town has a considerable affection for the Palmerston statue, though often treating it with casual respect. Footsteps were once painted from the statue to the Town Hall where public toilets were then located. At various times, he has sported a top hat, or his outstretched hand has received flowers or a lager can !

41   The Old Manor House, Palmerston Street, looking north c1865

Situated in historic Romsey Extra, the 'Old Manor House' belonged to the Fleming family as lords of the manor of Romsey Extra. It only became part of the Broadlands Estate after the enclosure agreements of 1807. Surprisingly little is known about this splendid timber-framed building, but the more northerly section is considered to be the older part, dating from the 16th century. Architectural details of the larger nearer section suggest that it belongs to the early 1600s. At the time of this photograph it was occupied by William Jeffrey, a well-known local farmer and contractor. The casual hold on the shot-gun by the gentleman in the picture (perhaps Mr Jeffrey himself) is rather alarming to the modern eye, but is a reminder of the rural element still present in late 19th-century Romsey.

42 The *Old Manor House*, 1999

The *Old Manor House* is now on the corner of Palmerston Street with Broadwater Road, the new throughway constructed in the 1960s. Today, the older part of this complex building is a private dwelling, while the major part, nearest the corner, is a well-established restaurant. The rendering on the restaurant was removed to reveal the brickwork in 1930, when the bricks had to be painstakingly reversed to hide the 'pecking' holes. These had been gouged out to enable the earlier plaster rendering to adhere properly.

43   Palmerston Street, with girls' procession, c1909

From Tudor times to the mid-19th century Palmerston Street was the start of the road to Southampton. Until the 1860s, it continued due south, passing rather close to Broadlands House. To secure greater privacy, Lord Palmerston seized the opportunity offered by the construction of the Andover-Southampton railway, and negotiated with the railway company for the re-routing of the road to its present more easterly line (see caption to picture 50). The truncated Tudor road to Southampton became known for a short while as Park Street, since it simply led to Broadlands Park with only comparatively minor ways off to east and west. It had been renamed Palmerston Street by the 1880s. Processions such as the one in this photograph were common along Palmerston Street, as various groups made their way for picnics in Broadlands Park.

44   Palmerston Street, 1999
The old Southampton road south of the Romsey by-pass is now a private road within Broadlands Park. After the opening of the by-pass in the 1930s, Palmerston Street regained its importance within the Romsey road system, especially when the by-pass was followed within thirty years by Broadwater Road. The latter road now links Palmerston Street with the bottom of Bell Street. Today, another sort of procession may frequently be seen in the form of a traffic jam !

45   Mitchell Bros at Fox Mill, c1900

Fox Mill was the last mill to be created in Romsey. It was built in 1799 as a corn-mill, utilising the water of the Tadburn Stream, on which it stood, augmented by waste water from the newly-opened Andover to Redbridge Canal. Rebuilt after a fire in about 1890, it was then sold to the nearby Broadlands Estate. It never operated as a mill again, but was occupied by a series of light industries. Mitchell Bros, a motoring business, turned to shell-making as a contribution to the First World War.

46   Fox Mill, 1999

Today, Fox Mill is adjacent to the busy Romsey by-pass, and is a private residential property. The name changed several times during its working life. It was once called Hundred Mill because it was approached from the north via a long entry from the Romsey street called The Hundred. It was also variously known as Soffe's Mill and Arnold's Mill after 19th-century millers there. 'Fox Mill' probably comes from the *Fox Inn* which once stood to the south just within the Broadlands stretch of the old Southampton road.

47   Gunville Gatehouse, Southampton Road, c1902

When the route to Southampton was changed in the 1860s (see caption to picture 43), Gunville Gatehouse was built as a new toll-house to serve the Southampton-Salisbury turnpike. (The site of an earlier toll-house for the Winchester turnpike is under the railway embankment at the junction of Winchester Road with Botley Road). The new toll-house had only a brief active life, as the turnpike trusts were wound up in the late 19th century. Local landowners usually had first option to purchase the toll-houses belonging to the defunct turnpike trusts, and consequently the gatehouse became part of the Broadlands Estate.

48   Gunville Gatehouse, 1999

The gatehouse is the only recognisable landmark in an area that is today dominated by a busy roundabout, the centre made more attractive by seasonal plantings and tall Lombardy poplars. A turning into a fairly recent side road, just beyond Gunville Gatehouse, is named Knatchbull Close. Knatchbull is the family name of Lord Romsey, who inherited Broadlands after the death of his maternal grandfather, Lord Mountbatten.

49   The Barge River and the Railway, 1920s

The Andover-Redbridge canal was built in the 1790s. Its success was short-lived, as its business was soon lost to the railways, which first came to Romsey in 1847, when the Eastleigh to Salisbury line was opened. Ironically, the approach to Romsey station crossed the canal on the bridge seen in the background. It was the second line, however, running from Andover to Southampton, that sounded the final knell for the canal. The company building this rail link during the 1860s actually bought up the old canal, filled it in, and constructed their line over it. Only the short stretch of canal at Romsey escaped, becoming a popular recreational area, locally known as The Barge River, or just 'The Barge'.

50   The Barge River, 1999

This section of the canal survives because the Andover-Southampton Railway Company, having bought up the canal for its route, took a more easterly line in Romsey as part of an overall agreement with Lord Palmerston of Broadlands. In exchange for land to be used by the railway further away to the east, Lord Palmerston benefited from both the diversion of the Southampton road away from Broadlands House and the building of the 'Mile Wall' around his park. It is now possible to walk the old canal towpath from the 'Plaza' roundabout northwards to Timsbury.

51   Winchester Road, looking west towards the junction with Alma Road, early 1900s
Richmond Terrace on the left was comparatively new at the time of this photograph. The business sign on the building to the right belonged to Maynard the coachbuilder. The rough surface of the road is a reminder that many key roads were still not made up at the beginning of the 20th century, although pavements gradually became a feature of Romsey following the setting up of a Pavement Commission in 1811.

52   Winchester Road, 1999

The Texaco petrol station on the right was undergoing major refurbishment at the time of this photograph. Just beyond it, the *Bishop Blaize* public house is now on the corner of the junction with Alma Road. The latter, taking its name from the Crimean War battle, was constructed in the mid-19th century to give easy access to the railway station from Broadlands. At the time of the old photograph there was another building, run as a veterinary practice, between the pub and the corner, but this disappeared in mid-20th-century street widening.

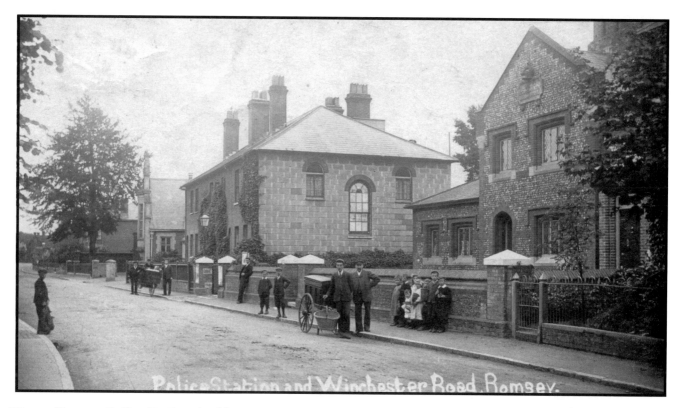

Police Station and Winchester Road, Romsey.

53   Romsey Police Station, looking east along The Hundred, c1908

Romsey Police Station was built in the mid-19th century, and features a splendid facade of dressed flints and bricks. Beyond, to the right of the large tree, is the British School, sponsored by the Nonconformist churches and opened in 1847. This building also has an interesting facade, reputedly designed by Parthenope Nightingale, sister of the famous Florence. (The Nightingale home was at Embley Park, Wellow.) The school faces down Alma Road.

54   Romsey Police Station, 1999

Romsey Police Station is the oldest building still serving as a police station within Hampshire. The British School subsequently became Romsey County Infants School, which closed in 1974. After a few years as a language school, it was converted into several dwellings under the collective name of English Court. Today, the street called The Hundred ends at the junction with Alma Road, and thereafter it is Winchester Road.

55   The Jam Factory, The Hundred, c1912

The timber-framed building to the left of the lady cyclist had its final incarnation as a jam factory. Many Romsonians remember earning pocket money for returning empty jars or, more dramatically, taking along a captured queen wasp, thus reducing the population of wasps that plagued the jam-makers. Furthermore, school log-books reveal a suspicious amount of truancy from local schools around blackberry-picking time !

The inset picture shows the interior of the jam factory in about 1910.

56   Waitrose, 1999

The jam factory closed in 1960, and remained derelict before it succumbed to fire in the mid-1960s. Waitrose Supermarket was built on the site soon afterwards, and has since expanded. The lay-out of the older buildings beyond is still recognisable. There is an awkward turn by these buildings as the road continues towards the Market Place, and this was probably caused in Tudor times by the need to create a new road to Southampton, via Palmerston Street, after Broadlands had become a private estate. The name of 'The Hundred' only dates from this time and relates to the fact that Romsey to the east of the Market Place was then in the civil administration of the Hundred (ancient county division) of Kings Somborne.

Latimer Street, Romsey.   A 5451.

57   Latimer Street from The Hundred, c1910

Latimer Street is one of the oldest streets in Romsey, with records dating back to the 13th century. At that time it seems to have been a high-status residential street with spacious plots. Property documents from the 18th-century indicate that much in-filling took place in Latimer Street during the 1700s. For example, the stretch from the turning on the near right, as far as the horse and wagon, was occupied by a single property in the 1720s, but had about nine dwelling-houses on the site by the end of the century. To the rear there was a path leading past the 'necessary house' (outside toilet) to a pig sty, and the side boundary was marked by a long gooseberry hedge, which may have stopped any pigs from straying in.

58   Latimer Street, 1999
Exterior paintings above the shop fronts on the right hand corner bear witness to the history of the butcher's shop that once thrived here. In 1995, the corner became an important part of the town as the Tourist Information Centre.

59   *The Rose & Crown*, Latimer Street, c1904/5

The landlord and his family outside *The Rose & Crown*. There were several public houses along Latimer Street, but only two now survive (*William IV* near the junction with Station Road and *The Romsey Tavern* at the junction with The Hundred). Some eighty Romsey buildings or sites have been identified as having been used as inns, public houses or ale-houses at some time in their history. *The Rose & Crown,* a fully licensed pub, can be dated back to 1784.

60   16 and 16A, Latimer Street, 1999

The Rose & Crown was one of a number of Romsey pubs that were closed during a purge of 1911. The purge followed the 1904 Balfour Licensing Act which enabled breweries to close the least successful of their over-numerous tied houses. At the time, Romsey had one public house for every 141 inhabitants, nearly twice the national average ! Once closed, *The Rose and Crown* building was subsequently occupied by a series of businesses, including a fish and chip shop and, more recently, a shop selling dress materials. At the time of writing, the shop is empty.

61   London Meat Market, The Hundred, c1912

The London Meat Market came to Romsey in the Edwardian era and lasted some seventy years. The building was designed by well-esteemed local architect, William Comley Roles, who also acted as clerk of works to Sir Edwin Lutyens. Iremonger's Basket Works lay just behind this building with side access. Basket-making has always been an unsung feature of most waterside settlements, but, for a brief period in the 1920s, Romsey boasted a high quality basket-making firm. Iremonger's manufactured perambulators, hampers and other fashionable basketry, selling most of its products through Harrod's.

62   New Look, 1999

The Meat Market building has been completely rebuilt. An archaeological excavation on the site, at the time of rebuilding, revealed an ancient ditch that may have been some sort of very early boundary. The high wall by the gap to the right still displays some old lettering and the residual marks of earlier roof lines, indicating the number of buildings that have been attached to it over the years. The tall property to which this high wall belongs was formerly *The Queen's Head*, one of Romsey's coaching inns. The upper windows feature interesting double-sashes, well worth an upward glance.

START
OF
WALK
THREE
Map and
directions at
back of book

63   Church Street, looking north from the Market Place, c1915

The buildings on the right side of Church Street, as far as the 'horseless carriage', had been rebuilt about forty years earlier as part of a road-widening project. The new row of shops was set further back, and a high-up commemorative stone reads *'Ashley Terrace 1880'*, the name coming from the Rt Hon. Evelyn Ashley of Broadlands. The average width of the street before the improvement was only 16 feet including the pavements. At its narrowest Church Street was only 13 feet across, making it impossible for two carriages to pass. The older properties on the left were untouched.

64   Church Street, 1999

The section of Church Street closest to the Market Place contains many shops, but the street becomes quieter and more residential further north. It is considered to be a key conservation area, especially as its west side follows the line of the old monastic boundary. No 2 Church Street, glimpsed on the extreme left with the 'For Sale' notice, has been identified as an important medieval timber-framed property behind its 18th-century facade. It suggests that the Abbey may have been improving its revenue by allowing building along its precinct boundary.

65   The Puckeridge Mansion, c1958, corner of Church Road and Church Place

The cottages in the foreground were built in about 1809 on the courtyard of the Puckeridge Mansion, a splendid house facing over Church Road to the old churchyard. It was probably built by Thomas Puckeridge in the early 18th century. His family fortune was based in the cloth industry that had brought prosperity to medieval Romsey. His son, Richard Puckeridge, died a bachelor in 1756 and it took twenty-one years to sort out the estate among his heirs, four sisters who were his cousins. The mansion deteriorated in the meanwhile, and became a warehouse. Part of it was eventually pulled down, while the surviving southern section, the taller building behind the right-hand cottages, was converted into two tenements facing onto Church Place.

66   Church Place, 1999

The cottages and tenements were demolished soon after the old view was taken. The site then became a temporary carpark until the Magistrates Court (now Social Services offices) was built in the 1960s. The modern building, seen from a slightly closer viewpoint than picture 65, faces onto Church Street with the Post Office opposite.

67   Site of Guard's Shop, Church Street west, c1890
Several elegant houses were built in Church Street during the Georgian period. This delightful example was demolished to make way for a new section (see inset) of the successful clothing shop run by the Guard family. The extended shop also included all the other buildings seen in the main photograph. The business had properties on both sides of the street, and this part was for menswear. Many older Romsonians particularly remember going to Guard's men's shop for boots and shoes.

68   Social Services offices, 1999
Schoolchildren had a narrow escape in the 1950s, when a corner of the menswear shop collapsed onto the pavement shortly after they had passed. Bad weather and the nearby underground stream had undermined the building, which then closed and soon became derelict. The building was pulled down as part of a wide-scale demolition to make way for the Magistrates Court in the 1960s. This building is now occupied by Social Services, the court function having been transferred to Lyndhurst.

69　King John's House to Romsey Abbey, 1908

This sketch appeared in the 1908 publication *Highways and Byways in Hampshire*. Drawn some twenty years before the reidentification of King John's House as an important 13th-century building, the accompanying text stated, rather ironically, that Romsey offered *'nothing to redeem it from utter commonplace'* apart from the Abbey. In fact, King John's House actually belonged to the Abbey at the time of the dissolution in 1539, but for how long and for what purpose is not known. Tree-ring dating and other evidence now suggests that the house was built in the 1250s. Thus it cannot be, as was once thought, the hunting lodge that King John built for himself in Romsey in about 1206.

70   King John's House, 1999
King John's House is now rightly seen as a building of tremendous historic significance and of great interest to visitors to the town. This important property now belongs to a trust that manages it on behalf of the townspeople, to whom it was endowed by the last owner, Miss A. M. A. Moody. There are no buildings remaining from which to obtain a view exactly comparable to the sketch.

71 Co-operative Store, Church Street, c1915
This view of the 'Co-op' Store in Romsey was taken when the chain's business was gathering momentum, and had yet to enter its most successful period. The terrace in which the shop was located is on the west side of Church Street. It was built in the late 1820s following a disastrous fire in 1826. During the 1960s Hampshire County Council, having built the Magistrates Court to the south, wished to demolish these houses to provide the site for a proposed new police station. This plan, however, never came to fruition.

72   Nos 22 to 28 Church Street, 1999
The building has survived, but, with the shop gone, it has been converted into a private residence (the central one of the three houses seen in this photograph). No. 30, just off the picture to the right, bears a plaque commemorating the birthplace of one of Romsey's most famous sons. Sir William Petty, *'Anatomist, Economist, Cartographer, Designer, Founder Member of the Royal Society'* was born in 1623 in a house formerly on this site. He was knighted by King Charles II, and was an ancestor of the Marquess of Lansdowne.

The Horsefair. Romsey.

73   The Horsefair, c1908
Heavily disguised under bunting, the public house on the left is *The Star*, formerly *The Swan & Dolphin*, and dating back to the 18th century. It was the site of a weaver's house in earlier days, and probably became a public house when the cloth trade declined in the south of England. The building on the right became offices of Romsey's great brewery, Strong & Co. Ltd. The main gates into the brewery premises were adjacent at right angles. It appears that the collection being made on this festive occasion was in aid of the local hospital, the subject of yet another appeal in 1999.

74   The Horsefair, 1999

The buildings in this scene are essentially unchanged and still pleasing to the eye. The street configuration, however, is somewhat puzzling. Its odd shape, and its position as a dog-leg between Church Street and Cherville Street, cannot be easily explained; and the name of The Horsefair does not help. The name can only be traced back to the mid-18th century, and even then - indeed, until the early 1800s - the area was always considered to be a part of Cherville Street.

75   Old Brewery Tower, Strong & Co. Ltd, The Horsefair, 1895

Strong's old brewery tower is an appropriate symbol for Romsey's brewing industry. This had begun to develop in the 18th century with the advent of common brewers who started to 'mass-produce' in a serious way. Their efforts were on a comparatively small scale, but marked a transition from the usual earlier practice, whereby individual innkeepers simply brewed for their own customers, on or off the premises. In the 1880s, David Faber created Strong & Co. Ltd from an amalgamation of several small local breweries. The brewery became very successful throughout Hampshire, owning several brewery sites and numerous public houses. The Horsefair site in Romsey was the focus of the business, and the archway over the main entrance bore the legend 'The Heart of the Strong Country'.

76 Horsefair House, 1999

The brewery tower was later extended westwards. Foundation stones for 1890 and 1929 may be seen on the respective sections. After a take-over by Whitbreads, brewing ceased in Romsey in 1981. Although a bottling and distribution business continued for a few years, all production work on the site ceased in 1988 when Whitbreads withdrew from the town. The key buildings have since been converted into small business centres and offices. Early in 1999, however, The Hampshire Brewery, based in Romsey, relaunched Strong's best bitter with the co-operation of Whitbreads. The statue of a horse in the foreground was a very recent addition to the Romsey scene at the time of this photograph, and cleverly reflects the name of The Horsefair.

CHERVILLE STREET. ROMSEY.

Sillence's
Photo. Serie

77   Cherville Street, looking north during World War I

Cherville Street takes the traveller north out of Romsey. It was probably a medieval planned 'suburb', though few of the existing buildings are older than the 18th century. There is a curious link, so far not fully explained, between this street and the manor of Rockbourne near Fordingbridge. Some properties had to make monetary payments to the lord of the manor of Rockbourne as late as the 18th century. An early holder of the manor of Rockbourne was Walter de Romsey, a very powerful man who may, perhaps, have been responsible for developing the street in the early 13th century. The eastern side of Cherville Street backs onto the Fishlake Stream, and the western side onto a back lane, which may represent a very early route. Recently, it has provided useful access to The Romsey School.

78   Cherville Street, 1999

There was considerable pressure to widen Cherville street during the 1960s, and properties were subsequently demolished or replaced along several short stretches. Nevertheless, the general atmosphere of the street remains the same. Once a very long thoroughfare, dwindling into countryside, its further reaches were redesignated as Greatbridge Road after the building of new houses in the 1920s. Curiously, though, the house numbers continue throughout, as if it were still a single street.

"THE OLD THATCHED COTTAGE" ROMSEY.

SILLENCE'S ROMSEY SERIES

79   *Old Thatched Cottage*, Mill Lane north side, c1905
The thatched cottage in Mill Lane had a long history as a brewery run for several generations by the Figes family. A succession of uncles and nephews were given the very distinctive name of Hatton Figes. By the 20th century, however, the *Old Thatched Cottage* was simply a beer-house, which lost its licence in 1918. Many similar places lost their licences at the beginning of the 20th century, and the rates of compensation seem very unfair. In this instance the licensee, Edward William Calley, received £80 while Strong & Co. Ltd, as the owners, received £660.

80   Thatched Cottage , 1999
Surrounded by a splendid hedge, Thatched Cottage is now a private residence. It is one of the very few thatched cottages remaining in Romsey.

Mill Lane, Romsey.

81   Mill Lane, looking west, c1905

Mill Lane can be dated back to the medieval period when it led to the watermills then owned by the Abbess of Romsey Abbey. Most of the houses along this route, however, date from more recent times. The terrace on the left, for example, known as Industry Row, was built for mill-workers in the early 19th century. The building on the far left corner was the *Delve Inn*, once one of Romsey's numerous public houses. It took its name from the nearby field of that name. The *Delve* had a discreet saloon for ladies and a bar for men, each with a separate entrance on different corners of the pub.

82　Mill Lane, 1999

Mill Lane is now a popular residential area with an interesting mixture of buildings. Further along from the old *Delve Inn* are 1930s' council houses built for people whose homes were in the way of the Romsey by-pass. On the far right of the lane in the photograph is a pleasant Victorian terrace. Beyond, and out of sight, is Volunteer Yard, a more recent development. It is named after the one-time beerhouse that was frequented by the Romsey Volunteers, whose practice range was beyond the end of Mill Lane. *The Volunteer*, a timber-framed single-storey building on the street front, has been incorporated into one of a group of new houses. Further on still is Mead Mill, on one of the medieval mill sites. It has been converted into a private museum, while the grounds have been developed as water gardens.

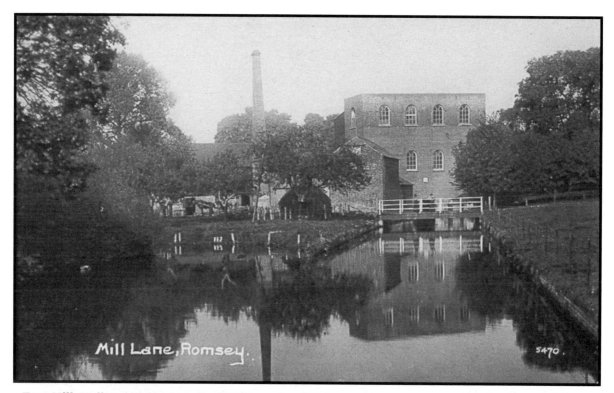

Mill Lane, Romsey.

5470.

83   Test Mill, Hollman Drive (north of Mill Lane), c1910

Test Mill was one of nine major mill-sites in Romsey, and was probably one of the first such sites to be developed. Nevertheless, its history is very obscure until the 18th century, when an old fulling mill was transformed for papermaking. Curiously, despite the antiquity of the site, the name 'Test Mill' has not been found in use before the 19th century, and no previous name is known. The building as seen here dates from the late 19th century when substantial renovations were made. Sadly, the owner responsible for these renovations, William Harvey senior, committed suicide shortly afterwards.

84   **Test Mill, 1999**

Test Mill was demolished in 1997 to make way for a private residential development. A commemorative stone from the mill was saved and inserted into the new building. It reads *'James Skeats 1706: William Harvey 1898'*, linking the names of two Romsey paper-makers. Another paper-maker at Test Mill, William Brookman, built the nearby Test House in the early 1800s.

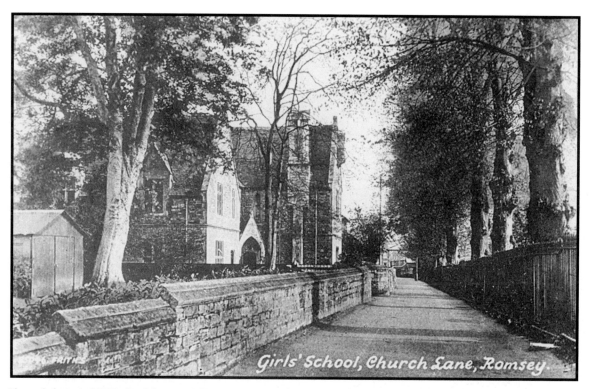

Girls' School, Church Lane, Romsey.

85   Church Lane, 1933, looking north

Church Lane, on the west side of the old churchyard, only really developed as a full link road in the mid-19th century. Previously there had been just a short spur off Mill Lane with houses on the west known as Delve Place and on the east as Spring Place. The extension of this lane was triggered by the building of the first purpose-built vicarage (of which a corner of the garden is seen on the far left) and, a few years earlier, the Girls' National School beyond. Confusingly, the name 'Church Lane' was previously used for the present Church Road together with Church Place.

86   Church Lane, 1999

The railings along the side of the churchyard were sacrificed for the war effort during the 1939-45 conflict, and the trees have been severely pollarded, but otherwise this view of Church Lane has changed very little. The vicarage is now a private house and the Girls National School has become the Romsey Abbey Primary School, the oldest building still serving as a school in Romsey.

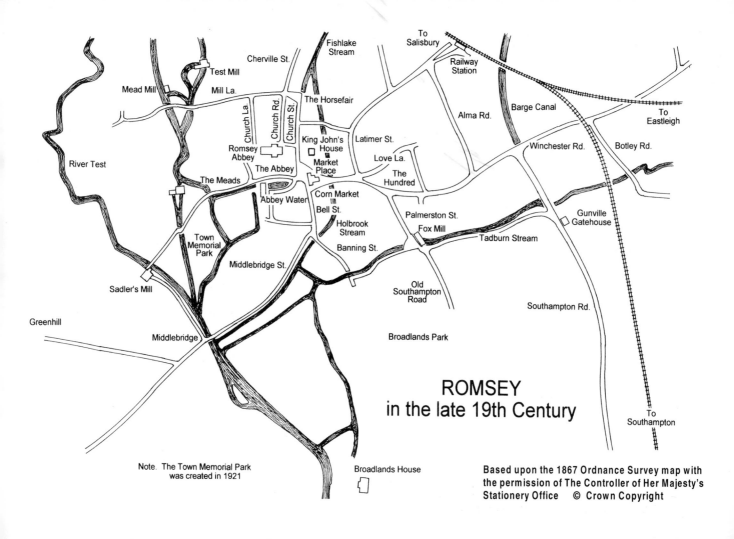

ROMSEY
in the late 19th Century

Note. The Town Memorial Park was created in 1921

Based upon the 1867 Ordnance Survey map with the permission of The Controller of Her Majesty's Stationery Office © Crown Copyright

WALK GUIDELINES, using picture numbers

(Where no instructions are given, continue in the same direction)

1 : START OF WALK ONE, from the corner of the Market Place with Church Street

2 >> 3 : Walk through the Market Place and a short distance down The Hundred (in the direction the statue is 'looking')

6 >> 7 : Turn back through the Cornmarket, turn right into Bell Street, then left into the Market Place again

12 >> 13 : Walk towards the Abbey gateway, turning left into Abbey Water just before you reach it

14 >> 15 : At the end of Abbey Water, turn right through an arch, right again, then left through a metal gate into the grounds of the Abbey.

18 >> 19 : Leave the Abbey by the same metal gate. Turn right carefully (no pavement) continuing straight down The Meads till you reach the Park

20 >> 21 : Leaving the Park by the main gate, turn left and follow the road, leading to a footpath through meadows to Sadler's Mill

22 >> 23 or 25 : If you wish to visit Greenhill for the next view, follow the footpath south-westwards across the fields. Otherwise, take the un-made-up riverside road from the Mill towards Middlebridge and the by-pass

26 >> 27 : Walk over Middlebridge and take the street that diverges left from the by-pass

From 28 : Follow Middlebridge Street and then Bell Street back to the Market Place. **This is the end of WALK ONE**

---

29 : START OF WALK TWO, leaving the Market Place and heading south down Bell Street

32 >> 33 : Continue down Bell Street

34 >> 35 : Bear left from Bell Street into Broadwater Road, then turn right into Banning Street

36 >> 37 : At the end of Banning Street, cross the Tadburn Stream by the footbridge. Decide between options (a) and (b) below

38 >> 39 or 41 : (a) To trace the 'rural footpath' alongside the Tadburn and/or visit Broadlands, turn left along the verge to the first roundabout. To visit Broadlands, cross the by-pass carefully at the roundabout. Later, return to the Palmerston Street turning off the same roundabout

(b) Retrace your steps to the town end of Banning Street and walk along Broadwater Road to Palmerston Street

44 >> 45 : From the Old Manor House walk southwards towards the by-pass and turn left onto the footpath that runs alongside the by-pass

46 >> 47 : Continue along the footpath, trying to ignore the traffic noise and to imagine this as a minor country lane leading to an 18th-century turnpike road with Gunville Gatehouse as the toll-house

48 >> 49 : Walk northwards towards the roundabout by the Plaza Theatre. Take the footpath that begins just to the left of the theatre

50 >> 51 : Retrace your steps to the Plaza roundabout, then turn right along Winchester Road, continuing into The Hundred

58 >> 59 : Walk a short distance up Latimer Street (right-hand turning)

60 >> 61 : Retrace your steps to The Hundred and turn right towards the town centre

From 62 : Walk back to the Market Place. **This is the end of WALK TWO**

---

63 : START OF WALK THREE, from the Church Street corner of the Market Place

64 >> 65 : Walk up Church Street, then turn left into Church Place

66 >> 67 : Return to Church Street, then cross to the Post Office

68 >> 69 : Explore King John's House and gardens (down the alley to the right of the Post Office)

70 >> 71 : Retrace your steps to Church Street and turn right

74 >> 75 : At the junction of Church Street with The Horsefair, turn right into the old brewery yard

76 >> 77 : Return to The Horsefair and walk just to the other end of this short 'street' where it turns right into Cherville Street

78 >> 79 : Keep on the same line as The Horsefair and continue west into Mill Lane

82 >> 83 : Continue along Mill Lane, then turn right into Hollman Drive

84 >> 85 : Return to Mill Lane (and, if you wish, explore its westerly section). Then walk back till you reach a right turn into Church Lane.

From 86 : Leave Church Lane, walking between the old churchyard and the north side of the Abbey. From Church Place turn right and walk back to the Market Place. **This is the end of WALK THREE**

ABOUT THE AUTHORS

Barbara Burbridge was born in Southampton and attended the Southampton Girls' Grammar School before reading history at London University. After graduating she worked for a short while in the City. Later, with two daughters both at school, she took her PGCE at Southampton University, and for the next fifteen years taught at Romsey Infants School. This was where she became interested in the local history of Romsey as part of the schoolchildren's environment. She joined the Lower Test Valley Archaeological Study Group (LTVAS) and became increasingly involved in its activities and research. Now retired, she is editor of the LTVAS newsletter and of its major publications, and represents the group on several outside bodies. She is co-author of *'The Story of Romsey'* and editor and co-author of *'Romsey Mills & Waterways'*. Local history has also led her into the very absorbing study of medieval Latin.

Gerald Ponting was born in Breamore, near Fordingbridge, and attended Bishop Wordsworth's School, Salisbury. Following study at the Universities of Southampton and Leicester, Gerald's career as a biology teacher took him first to Suffolk. There he began to take an interest in local history, researching and writing the history of Kesgrave, near Ipswich. During ten years in the Outer Hebrides, he wrote a number of books about the Standing Stones of Callanish and lectured on the topic in the U.S.A. He received a British Archaeological Award for researches at Callanish. On returning to Hampshire, he taught at The Burgate School, Fordingbridge, for eight years, until his early retirement. Gerald is now a Blue Badge Tourist Guide and a free-lance writer, photographer and lecturer. With Anthony Light, he has written and published ten books and booklets on local history in the Fordingbridge area. *'Chandler's Ford – Yesterday and Today'*, compiled with Barbara Hillier and uniform with this volume, was published in 1998.